ETERNAL COSMIC WISDOM

AT

BARGAIN BASEMENT PRICES

Why Pay More?

Jerry D. Posner

Eternal Cosmic Wisdom at Bargain Basement Prices

ISBN-13: 978-1466214392

BISAC Headings:
SEL016000 SELF-HELP / Personal Growth / Happiness
SEL021000 SELF-HELP / Motivational & Inspirational

Cover design by Jen Odegaard

"Simplicity is the ultimate sophistication."

Leonardo DaVinci

"You are perfect as you are, and you could use a little work."

Shunryu Suzuki-Roshi

"Is every book of wisdom simply a rehash of every other book of wisdom? Yeah, probably. Not that there's anything wrong with that!"

Jerry D. Posner

"Wisdom is plentiful. Applied wisdom perhaps less so. A little bit of the applied kind can go a long, long way."

Jerry D. Posner

Eternal: enduring and boundless

Cosmic: vast and limitless

Wisdom: intelligence and common sense

Bargain Basement Prices: excellent cost/benefit ratio

- A PRACTICAL, MODERN TWIST ON SOME OLD STANDARDS!

- EXPANDED AWARENESS—NO WAITING!

Alignment Jobs • Reframing Service • Mood Management Magic

- AMAZE YOUR FRIENDS AND CONFOUND YOUR ENEMIES … ESPECIALLY THE ENEMY WITHIN!

- DISCOVER YOUR OWN CONFIRMATION BIASES!

- BECOME AN ESCAPE ARTIST FROM SELF-DELUSION PRISON!

- GREAT IDEA-VIRUSES THAT YOU'LL <u>WANT</u> TO BE INFECTED WITH!

- OLD BROMIDES PROVOKING SMART CHOICES!

Presenting a collection of practical, helpful suggestions and reminders to make life better, have more fun, get more done, love more.

ALTERNATIVE TITLES:

Brain, Heart, and Courage

Little Daily Miracles

What's Really Important to Me Now?

Simple Wisdom for Complicated People

The Placebo Wizard

How's That Workin' For You?

What, Why, How?

Wisdom: Pure, Simple, and Potent

When It Works, Keep Doing It

Bite-Sized Nuggets of Smartness

Table of Contents

Thanks, Professors!

This book is dedicated to my wife, partner, best friend, and live-in coach Lynne Paige Posner, who helped me recognize that old dogs *can* learn new tricks and that love does indeed trump everything.

And to my parents Hy and Irene Posner, who have loved and supported me my whole life, no matter what weird or nutty stuff I was doing.

To our canine companions, Rubles Toomuchova (Ruby) and Maxwell C. Posner, thank you for your love, devotion, and entertainment. Woof!

To all my friends, family, clients, colleagues, and community ... much gratitude and deep appreciation for all that you've done to support my life's mission, making the butterfly effect work for me. Special thanks to Susan Russell, John and Dave Pelletier, John Mathers, Scott Schiff, Karen Davis, Nick Boulas, Canyon Ranch in the Berkshires, Don and Jackie Wescott, Jayne Church, and Jess Kielman.

A huge cheer of appreciation to the schoolteachers, college professors, and guidance counselors who've pursued their passion to encourage and guide our growth and development. Let us not forget them. Friend them on Facebook and say, "thanks!"

To my editor, Victoria Wright, at BookmarkServices.net, thanks and great job as usual!

And thank *you* for reading this book. It's dedicated to you, as well.

"Every day is a good day because you're in it."

JDP

Some of the essays in this book were originally published in the *Cabrito Gazette* and Jerry Posner's blog: *Improvement — The Easy Ways.*

This is Volume Two in the *Practical Wisdom in Easy-To-Digest, Bite-sized Nuggets* trilogy. Volume One, *Attention Late Bloomers: You're Right On Time* was released in 2006.

There are four principal areas of focus in this book (and in my life):

1. Practical application of the butterfly effect

2. Ways to create miracles in your life.

3. Practicing the practical power of gratitude

4. Love trumps everything

Dear Reader,

Does profound, transformative wisdom have to be complicated, arcane, nebulous and, so often, *expensive*? Of course not. Keep It Simple, Sweetie!

I love the small reminders that encourage me to:

> Make better choices
>
> Keep things in perspective
>
> Behave in an authentic and kind way
>
> Feel and express more love and gratitude
>
> Have fun
>
> Manage my moods and stress before they manage me
>
> Communicate clearly, accurately, kindly, effectively
>
> Choose balance instead of freaking out
>
> Remember my motivations
>
> Get off my butt and DO SOMETHING!

Consider the concise elegance and wisdom of these old proverbs and sayings.

As you do, *put a checkmark next to the ones you really want to remember.*

Review daily ... and see what happens after a month or so.

_____ Don't judge a book by its cover.

_____ What goes around comes around.

_____ Be careful what you wish for ... you might get it.

_____ Let sleeping dogs lie.

_____ A stitch in time saves nine.

_____ Actions speak louder than words.

_____ Plan your work ... and work your plan.

_____ One bad apple spoils the whole bunch.

_____ A penny saved is a penny earned.

_____ Don't get wet before it rains.

_____ Before you lose your temper, count to ten.

_____ What the thinker thinks, the prover proves.

_____ You can't get to the top by sitting on your bottom.

_____ Birds of a feather flock together.

_____ Don't put all your eggs in one basket.

_____ Love makes the world go round.

_____ Love doesn't make the world go round. Love is what makes the ride worthwhile. (attributed to Franklin P. Jones or Franklin P. Adams)

_____ Haste makes waste.

_____ As you sow, so shall you reap.

_____ Boys will be boys.

_____ Same meat, different gravy.

_____ Do unto others as you would have them do unto you.

Lots of variations on the Golden Rule theme ...

_____ Never impose on others what you would not choose for yourself.

(Confucius)

_____ Avoid doing what you would blame others for doing.

(Thales)

_____ That which is hateful to you, do not do to your fellow.

(Hillel, Talmud)

_____ Love your neighbor as yourself.

(Leviticus)

_____ Do not do unto others as you would that they should do unto you. Their tastes may not be the same.

(George Bernard Shaw)

Simple Wisdom Works ... When We Apply It!

If you choose your battles wisely, will your life be better? Will you be happier?

If you think before you speak, will your relationships be smoother? Will you experience less stress?

If you make your choices based on the outcomes you most desire, will you be more aware of potential choices ... and more aware of exactly what outcomes you DO desire? Might we make BETTER choices and have MORE successful outcomes with this perspective?

If you keep a gratitude journal (every day, write five things that are good in your life), will you have a happier life? Will you forgive others, and yourself, easier? Will you feel better? Kinder? More secure? Will your immune system function more efficiently?

Can old proverbs and clichés trigger effective thinking and smart choices?

Did our grannies actually possess the deep wisdom we seek?

Maybe so—if we REMEMBER those little sayings ... repeat or reinforce them enough to

affect our behavior, decisions, and habits …
and thus, modify cause-and-effect chains in a
positive way—potentially stacking the odds in
our favor.

I have a collection of handy reminders to share with you.

Simple and powerful.

I approach my subject as an interested party,
not as an academic, theologian, medical
professional or guru of any kind.

 I offer an all-you-can-eat idea buffet. You
don't have to eat everything, just the "food for
thought" that you like most!

I want you to have a good time reading this
book. Keep an open mind … but not SO open
that your brains fall out.

Think for yourself, experiment wisely, watch
for results, learn from experience, and have as
much fun as you can.

Gratefully,

Jerry

Recognize the idea or exercise that you strongly suspect will get you the results you desire.

Remember it (to-do lists, little cards with focus-phrases, visualizations, etc.).

Reinforce regularly with focused attention and action (disciplined practice and performing the necessary work). As you progress, pay close attention to feedback, adjust your plan as necessary—and, voila!

Visiting the Happy Place

This Positivity Research Project was initially inspired by an act of violence. It was a brutal mugging by three drugged-up miscreants in a neighbor's Boston apartment, on the eve of my twenty-third birthday. After I grasped the fact that I had survived a seemingly close encounter with the Reaper, I was unusually anxiety-free and happy for a couple of weeks or so. Grateful. Giddy.

Then I returned to baseline. Not horrible by any means, but not exactly optimistic either. My everyday personality contained substantial portions of drama, anxiety, emotional insecurities, and unwise choices. After all, I was a 23-year-old human male.

However, the "happy place" I briefly inhabited fascinated me. I liked the feeling and wondered if it was possible to return, perhaps to live there permanently! I began researching and studying ways that people become more positive, happier, and successful. I experimented with many philosophies, approaches, and methods, aiming to learn practical, actionable techniques for positive growth and change. Some of these techniques were complicated, vague, and dogmatic.

Others were ridiculously simple—just garden-variety common sense and easily applied.

Over time, I succeeded.

And I concluded that simple stuff seemed to work the best for me.

Brain. Heart. Courage.

Remember? From *The Wizard of Oz*?

The Scarecrow. The Tin Man. The Cowardly Lion.

Representing:

- Mental focus. Emotional focus. Brave action.

- Right mental attitude. Right emotional attitude. Appropriate risktaking.

- Knowing. Wanting. Doing.

Employ all three—create the future more elegantly.

Employ all three—make improvements more easily.

Mental focus:

What do I pay attention to?

What do I notice?

What do I ignore?

What do I remember?

Emotional focus:

What do I strongly desire?

What feelings do I want to feel?

What generates enthusiasm?

What are my emotional motivations?

Action:

How do I behave?

How do I communicate?

How do I treat people ... and myself?

What do I do?

BRAIN + HEART + COURAGE = WHAT?

Nice little formula!

Fortunately, the wizard is YOU.

YOU'RE the person behind the curtain!

And remember, you've ALWAYS had the power to return to Kansas!

WHAT'S GOING ON IN THERE?

Let's pay some close attention to our thoughts. At this moment ... right NOW... what's going on in there? What do you notice? The words on this page? The weather? The music playing in the background? Your desire for another cup of coffee?

What do you remember, and what do you forget?

What interpretations and connections are you making consciously *and* unconsciously?

You could be thinking about a million different things. Is your thinking on purpose, or on automatic pilot? Are "you" the observer or creator ... or both at once?

Some thoughts inspire you. Some are neutral. Some energize. Some delight you! Some depress you. Some are productive. Others, not so much.

Thoughts are important links in the chains of cause and effect.

Thoughts trigger feelings.

Each moment there are a gazillion thoughts to choose from. Pick some good ones!

Think the thoughts that point you in the right direction. This often involves practice.

These elementary bits o' wisdom are as old as the hills … yet, there are still people who regularly practice "stinking thinking"—daily—and don't realize they're doing it. Do you know anyone like that? Yeah, me too. Pessimists make miracles also—in reverse!

Let's be students of cause and effect … and take some good notes along the way.

Let's be excellent observers of our thoughts.

Let's be better listeners.

Then we'll have more information.

Then we'll make better choices!

That would be excellent!

How much would that cost?

That's right, nothing.

Cliché alert:

We can't change what we don't notice.

Does Everything Happen For a Reason?

"Some people want it to happen, some wish it would happen, others make it happen."

Michael Jordan

A common saying, one I see on Facebook all the time, is:

Everything happens for a reason.

Just ONE reason? I don't think so. I'd say LOTS of reasons! Way too many reasons to know *all* of them, but we sure can know *some* of them—and that would certainly be helpful!

I'm sure you've noticed that some events and circumstances in your life are completely out of your control, some you can and do control, and some are in the *maybe* state—the *you never know* state—the *could be* state.

For example: I AM HERE NOW

1. Because I was born.

2. Because my parents were born, they met, and … well, you know.

3. Because my grandparents were born, they met, etc.

4. Because I'm just drawn that way (*Who Framed Roger Rabbit*).

5. Because of my childhood experiences.

6. Because I made a choice to be here now.

7. Because I made a gazillion other choices, too.

8. Because I have habits.

9. Because Planet Earth supports lifeforms like me.

Numbers 1, 2, and 3 are "no control" events.

Numbers 4 and 5 might be considered "maybe state."

Numbers 6, 7 and 8 are within our control (habits can be made or broken).

Number 9 is miraculous, when you think about it.

Take a minute and make your own list.

I AM HERE NOW BECAUSE ...

_____

_____

_____

_____

_____

Good Luck? Law of Attraction? Karma? Random Chance?

Who the Hell Knows For Sure, Anyway?

A local music store announced a raffle for a really nice acoustic guitar. I'm particularly fond of quality musical instruments and I also like supporting this particular business, so I bought six tickets—a total investment of $25.

I thought this would be an ideal opportunity to experiment with mind-over-matter-style positive thinking. Though I tend to be a rationalist in these matters, I do like to keep an open mind (and flexible belief system). And besides, making magic is fun!

Here's exactly what I did before the guitar drawing:

I declared to my wife that I was going to win. She supported that possibility.

I imagined I'd be the winner. I visualized myself walking out of the store with the guitar in my hand, smiling.

I stated to the cosmos (and to myself) that I deserved to win at least as much as anyone, so it might as well be me.

In my pocket, a tiny statue of Lakshmi, the Hindu Goddess of abundance—a customary "good luck" talisman.

One hour before the raffle, I strolled around the neighborhood of the music store, thinking positive thoughts and feeling how wonderful it would feel when I won. I also ate an ice cream cone, adding another pleasurable, albeit caloric, emotional element to the mix.

I finished the ice cream (delicious), arrived at the music store, and was told there were about 200 tickets sold. I figured my statistical odds were decent, making me feel even more confident.

Right before the drawing, Sean, one of the owners, joked, "how about if you give me 10 bucks and I'll draw your name?" I told him I didn't have to give him 10 bucks because he was going to draw my ticket anyway. He laughed. I entered a meditative state, imagining I was at one with the universe, which included the bowl of tickets, Sean's hand and "my" guitar.

Sean took off his sweater, indicating "nothing up my sleeve." He reached into the bucket, and... BINGO, I'm the winner!

I thanked the clearly flabbergasted Sean and walked to my car with the prize—the exact scene I had imagined.

So, what happened? Did I affect the outcome with my positive thinking and ritual ... or was my winning just random chance? Was this "future causation" or simply really good luck? Destiny? Karma?

What do you think?

And if the quantum field can indeed be manipulated, how come there aren't more psychic lottery winners? And who says that there aren't?

What do *I* think? I think, "I don't know for sure, but I sure like to experiment with this stuff!"

If I believe in Guardian Angels, will they protect me?

Will Saint Anthony help me find my lost keys?

Does the Hamsa ward off the evil eye?

Can a rose quartz amplify feelings of love?

Should I allow extra travel time during a Mercury retrograde period?

When a belief is helpful … and harmless … and may increase the likelihood of positive outcomes … then, why not?

Wisdom in a Word

Listen.

What's Important To Me Now?

Good question.

What do I want to do?
What do I want to improve?
What do I want to feel?
What do I want to have?

> Happiness?
>
> Prosperity?
>
> Skills mastery?
>
> Peace and calm?
>
> Better health?
>
> Loving relationships?
>
> Meaningful career?
>
> Creativity without limits?
>
> Spiritual connection?
>
> More moolah?

Jot down a few answers of your own:

_____

_____

_____

_____

_____

Would you consider any of THOSE to be a miracle?

Research strongly suggests that miracles do happen …

sometimes with a simple change of perspective—other times with disciplined work.

I'm mostly interested in the miracles that we create, the "unusual splendid outcomes" that we consciously manifest.

Miracles begin with a first step.

It could be just a little baby step … in the right direction, of course!

"A whole lot of littles makes a whole lot of lots."

Stevie Wonder

D.I.Y. MIRACLES

"Every moment of light and dark is a miracle."

Walt Whitman

"Everything is a miracle. It is a miracle that one does not dissolve in one's bath like a lump of sugar."

Pablo Picasso

"It is a miracle that curiosity survives formal education."

Albert Einstein

"To be alive, to be able to see, to walk, to have houses, music, paintings—it's all a miracle."

Arthur Rubinstein

"Miracles happen everyday, change your perception of what a miracle is and you'll see them all around you."

Jon Bon Jovi

In my previous book, *Attention Late Bloomers: You're Right On Time*, I wrote a few chapters on the subject of miracles, and shared some ways of increasing the likelihood of these seemingly low-probability, positive outcomes … sometimes called *miracles.*

Since then, I have received lots of helpful feedback from readers and workshop attendees, sharing what has worked best for them.

Want to create a specific miracle in YOUR life? Or perhaps you'd just like to become a bit more *miracle-prone*?

Good. you've come to the right place! This is the revised version.

But first, let's discuss "miracles" in general …

What is a miracle?

There are lots of definitions and interpretations of that word. Here are a few:

- a miracle is a wonderful occurrence

- a miracle is unusual (from the perspective of the observer)

- a miracle may seem to defy the known laws of physics

- a miracle is a very positive outcome that seems low-probability based on available information and experience

- a miracle is a positive, good thing

IDENTIFYING THE ACTUAL SOURCE OF THE MIRACLE CAN BE A MATTER OF FAITH and SPECULATION

There are different varieties of miracles. Like the gift miracles which appear to happen through no effort or awareness of our own. And the deliverance miracle—when we're delivered from imminent danger or disaster—a near miss, so to speak—and we can't comfortably explain how it happened.

The word "miracle" has various meanings and associations.

"Childbirth, now that's a miracle!"

"Passing my test would be a miracle."

"It's a miracle! Thank you, God."

"I got married. My parents still say it was a miracle!"

"My computer is a miracle. My iPad2 is an even bigger miracle."

"It would be a miracle to be happier—just a little happier, that's all I ask.

"If I stopped complaining—THAT would be a miracle!"

"She's a miracle worker!"

"It was a miracle of science."

"New washday miracle!"

Of course, there have been, and still are, events called medical miracles, healing miracles, right place/right time miracles, miracles of love and compassion. Business miracles. Miracles of opportunity. Creativity miracles. Miracles of awareness. Maybe you're having one right now.

We might associate miracles with meaningful coincidence or synchronicity. Good luck and good karma also come to mind.

I'd classify Olympic figure skaters' performances as miracles. To my mind, Shawn White mocks gravity and sidesteps the laws of physics! The recordings of The Beatles, Yo-Yo Ma, Stevie Wonder, Brian Wilson, and Frank Zappa—are miraculous achievements of virtuosity and creativity. How about Babe Ruth? Mozart? Banksy? Gandhi? Spielberg? Oprah? Dylan? Madonna? B.B. King? Steve Martin? J.K. Rowling? Lady Gaga? Warren Buffet? They started creating their miracles the same way we do … at the beginning.

"I have plans that are unbelievable. But then wanting to be a guitar player seemed unbelievable at one time."

Jimi Hendrix

Jimi, you really nailed it.

Dear reader, how many "miracles" do you have in your life right now that you once considered near impossible?

We're on the BRAIN-HEART-COURAGE journey from *unconscious incompetence* to *conscious incompetence*, to *conscious competence*, and, having mastered the desired skills and having co-created the circumstances, ending up in the wonderful *unconscious competence* zone … becoming miracle-prone, as it were! Imagine that your individual path of success, happiness and gratitude becomes habit. Wouldn't *that* be a miracle worth creating?

Redundant Cliché Alert.

Our journey begins with the first step.

Let's set one small or medium sized miracle-goal now, and start our own chains of cause and effect moving on down the line!

BUT BEFORE YOU UNLEASH THE COSMIC POWER TO MANIFEST YOUR MIRACLES …

Take a moment now to review some **specific THINGS and CONDITIONS you want most in your life**, and ask yourself, "Is that possible for me? How important is it to me? Why do I want it?" Self-awareness can be miraculous, too.

Think carefully and jot a few down.

SOME THINGS AND CONDITIONS I WANT MOST IN MY LIFE:

_____

_____

_____

_____

_____

For now, pick just one positive outcome (or goal) in a life area of your choosing.

A change for the better.

It might be acquiring a material thing … some relationship-tweaking … skills mastery … task achievement … spiritual service … attitude adjustment … mood management, etc. Choose an outcome (or goal) that is important to you and, ideally, emotionally fulfilling as well.

WHAT'S REALLY IMPORTANT TO ME NOW?

You might want to write that question out on a card or sticky-note, read it every day, and ponder the meaning for a minute or two. Daily.

One theory of mine about miracle making:

Large miracles often begin with a choice or action that appears small and insignificant at first.

I call this the **Little Bang Theory,** also known as the Butterfly Effect.

For example: if a butterfly flutters its wings in Michigan, a cause-and-effect chain can become activated that eventually results in a major windstorm in the Berkshires. That windstorm knocks out the electricity, so people in the bars can actually hear each other schmooze, and thus, a relationship between two lonely people is formed that would not have been, and they eventually fall in love, get married ... and a child is born ... who grows up to discover a biotechnology breakthrough that eventually saves the life of an inventor who develops a machine that milked the cow with the crumpled horn, that tossed the dog that worried the cat, that killed the rat that ate the malt, that lay in the house that Jack built.

But what if that particular butterfly is captured and brought to the butterfly house at the Bellagio in Las Vegas? Then what happens to the universe? What about that biotech breakthrough? Is everything different now? Really? A little butterfly, for God's sake!!! How can this be?

How important IS that particular little butterfly?

What if George Bailey was never born?

What if Columbus discovered Australia?

What if your maternal grandparents never met?

What if you never found this book?

If a "little something" participates in creating "something big," then that "little something" isn't little at all. It's crucial. And "little somethings" are so much easier to manage.

Suggestion:

Recognize and identify the miracles you have in your life now, and ponder their many causes. Take notes, and feel the gratitude.

If I wanted to inhabit a particular future that contains my miracles, clearly there are things I can do to *increase* their likelihood … and there are things I can do to *decrease* it.

A simple, powerful reminder: **"I make my choices based on the outcomes I desire."**

Every day I give the wheel of fortune a spin with my:

- thoughts
- feelings

- actions
- choices
- habits
- beliefs
- attention
- intention
- communications
- attitudes
- expectations

That just about covers it.

What can I control? ... What is beyond my control? ... And what's in the *maybe state*? Let's primarily work with the factors in our control, leave the beyond-control stuff alone, and have some fun with the *maybe state*.

Cliché alert.

Everything affects everything.

"Remember there's no such thing as a small act of kindness. Every act creates a ripple with no logical end."

Scott Adams

Links In the Chains of Causation

Gary is divorced and living in New Jersey. He decides to attend his high school reunion. Initially, he didn't want to go, but his mom convinced him. At the reunion he meets an old friend whom he hadn't seen in forty years. The friend is a Broadway producer and currently has a hit play. He invites Gary to attend his play as his guest. Gary usually opts out of this kind of activity, but he was a little drunk, so he said, "Okay."

Plans are made to attend.

He takes the train to New York City and the subway to the theatre, where he discovers that the box office botched the reservation and doesn't have his tickets. The performance is completely sold out.

So cursing his rotten luck, and annoyed that he made the trip for nothing, he heads back to the subway. As he approaches the station, he remembers that he skipped breakfast and lunch, which he hardly ever did in the past, so he's especially hungry. Gary walks into a nearby restaurant and sits down.

The server, Elaine, is a new hire and not performing well. Gary, still in a foul mood from the ticket screw-up, becomes visibly peeved at the lack of competence, and coldly requests another server. Elaine takes this rejection to heart, bursts into tears, hands in her apron and resigns on the spot. (The next week, she will move back to Ohio, find a much better job and meet a great guy...).

Gary's new waitress is Claire, experienced and top-notch. He has such a good time speaking with her, enjoying the exemplary service, that he eats and drinks more than usual, staying in the restaurant much longer than planned.

Now the restaurant is closing. Gary pays the cashier, and as he's leaving, he sees that Claire is leaving too, so they walk together to the subway.

Now, what if ...

Gary dates Claire, falls in love, and marries her?

Gary is mugged and becomes an advocate for victim's rights? (And meets his future wife at a City Hall demonstration.)

Gary finds a wallet on the sidewalk and receives a $1000 reward, invests the dough in a promising biotech stock, gaining an additional $2000, and pays off a debt that has been worrying him for months?

Gary goes home, gets drunk, and writes a hit song?

Gary joins A.A.?

What if …

Gary stayed home?

That's right! EVERYTHING (in this story) would surely be different!

One door closes and a gazillion other ones open. We walk through one and it closes … and a gazillion more open. Rinse. Repeat.

Each and every one of the "many little things" in this story can be seen as a vital link in the chain of cause and effect. I don't see this chain as linear—more like the way billiard balls scatter when you break with the cue ball. The balls go in many different directions—some predictable, some perhaps not.

So, maybe everything *does* affect everything, in some ways predictable … and others not.

Choose one particularly wonderful event or outcome in your life that, looking back, you might classify as a miracle. What do you think was the tipping point? What made it happen? Perhaps everything that ever happened contributed to this miracle. Or not. Maybe some metaphysical positive-thinking power … or random chance. Maybe prayers were answered. Maybe the placebo effect. Maybe it's all smoke and mirrors. Might it be part of some huge master plan? Perhaps a happy accident.

Interesting to ponder that stuff, but I'm more interested in making miracles then trying to explain them.

A Synchronicity Story

On a rainy Wednesday, Lynne and I decided to go to MASS MoCA (Massachusetts Museum of Contemporary Art) in North Adams as a part of our second wedding anniversary celebration. We were going to go to the museum first thing in the morning, then have lunch as Jae's Inn, also in North Adams, but we changed our minds and chose lunch first, museum later.

At lunch, I noticed a woman working there who looked familiar. It turned out she was the daughter of an old friend of mine, also working there. I hadn't seen the daughter or her mom in sixteen years, so we had a lovely chat. The mom also figured into a chance conversation I had with the manager of the Holiday Inn in Salem, New Hampshire ... but that's another story.

So, after that unexpected reunion, Lynne and I headed to the museum. While we were in line to pay for admission, we heard a young couple laughing because, as the guy shook off his umbrella, his wedding ring fell off of his finger and rolled onto the floor. The woman mentioned something about how funny this was, the ring falling off on this, their wedding anniversary. And yes, it was also their second.

What are the odds of two couples celebrating their second wedding anniversaries on the exact same day, standing next to each other at the exact same time in line at MASS MoCA?

And, of course, we wouldn't have known about their anniversary, if the guy's ring didn't fall off of his finger at that precise moment!

Timing.

So, as in all synchronicities or "low-probability meaningful events" there are many factors that conspire to create the result. Right place at the right time suggests that every little decision, all delays, traffic flow, chance meetings, etc., can create or put the kibosh on any possible result.

Do you enjoy experiencing these meaningful coincidences? If so, keep a log or journal of them ... you'll probably notice—or create— many more of them!

<u>Wisdom in a Word</u>

Compassion.

Some Ways To Create Miracles In YOUR Life

Here's a three-step process with a fine track record and many revisions!

Step One: Pick a miracle—a positive outcome in some area of your life that is important to you. It could be about business, relationships, finance, family, personal growth, creativity. I'd suggest a small or medium-sized miracle—those are much easier to create! Write it down.

Step Two: Make sure you really want it.

Ask yourself "Brain—Heart—Courage" questions, such as:

- What are my thoughts about this miracle? Are they positive? Conflicted?

- Can I imagine it, and imagine the impact to my life?

- How much do I want it?

- Does the thought of it make my heart sing?

- Do I have the courage to act? To risk disappointment?

- Do I have the courage to ask for it? To accept it?

If you're happy with your answers, then proceed to …

Step Three: Eight suggestions or reminders to be practiced, in some appropriate combination, DAILY!

- Visualize the outcome … and the path to it. Visualize the steps you need to take. Break it up into small, smart actions. Also visualize yourself calmly dealing with potential obstacles and solving problems that could come up.

- Desire it. Maintain enthusiasm, excitement, and emotional focus.

- Anticipate it. Expect it. Believe in it. Some miracles require faith, hope, and patience.

- Ask for assistance and accept the help when it is offered. Networking, emotional support, cheerleaders, prayer, Google, mentors …

- Put your miracle on your to-do list. Remind yourself daily.

- Choose optimism and remember your motivations—your reasons for wanting to create this miracle.

- Give yourself permission to have it. You just might be the one blocking it! Need more deserve-ability? Simply take a file card, write or print PERMISSION SLIP on it. Meditate on the card for a minute or two every day. By the way, you do not have to be a perfect person in order to create a miracle. There's not one person who has ever received or created a miracle who is a perfect person.

• Make a plan, adjust as necessary. Be aware of feedback that comes from others, and from your own observations. Evaluate feedback WITHOUT becoming defensive! Enjoy the process!

PUT YOUR MIND TO IT.

PRACTICE.

STAY THE COURSE.

"There are many millions of people who would say that most everything about your life, right now, is a miracle. Are you one of them?"

JDP

Why?

Why are we where we are right now?
1. **Choices.**
2. **Habits.**
3. _____ **(fill in the blank)**

Our audience said ...

- Consequences
- Contracts
- Circumstances
- Mistakes
- Passion
- Karma
- Love and luck
- Opportunities and awareness of them
- Fate
- Goals
- The Devil (LOL!)
- Selective attention
- Intentions

- Kismet

- Fear

- Money

- Acceptance

- Significant other

- Beliefs

- Security

- Attitude

- All of the above

How would you fill in the blank?

_____

Wha' Happened?

I was giving a lecture at Canyon Ranch some years back, writing, "If you could create a miracle in your life ... what might it be?" on the whiteboard, and my right arm suddenly froze up, hurting like hell! Really, it was incredibly painful and I couldn't raise it no matter how hard I tried. Since I'm not exactly a sports or exercise enthusiast, I had no idea what this was or how it happened. *Bummer!*

I told my mom, who suggested, "Maybe you've been strumming your ukulele too hard." I replied, "Is that what you call it these days?" (Variation on an old joke, please forgive me.)

The next morning, I saw my physician who immediately sent me to the local orthopedist, who took some x-rays and pronounced, "You have a torn rotator cuff."

Me: "What does this mean?"

Doc: "You're going to need surgery."

Me: "Won't it just heal?"

Doc: "No, it needs to be sewn up."

Me: "I don't think I want surgery."

Doc: "If you don't get surgery, you'll regret it."

I reluctantly scheduled the surgery and began regular physical therapy, as the doctor said it would help ease the pain and eventually enable me to move my arm, at least. The therapy actually increased the pain, but modern pharmacology helped with that.

I have many caring friends with a multitude of belief systems. Advice was freely and lovingly offered. "Visualize white light in your shoulder." "Chant this healing mantra."

Spiritually-oriented friends were praying for me, and some put me on prayer lists. There were people I never met in the Midwest saying prayers for my rotator cuff. Atheists were sending me positive thoughts. I was appreciating all the concern and kind wishes.

A Christian friend suggested, "Why not ask Jesus to help you?"

I replied, "Uh … because I'm Jewish?"

"So was Jesus."

"Okay, what do I do?"

"You like to visualize, right? Just imagine that Jesus has his hand on your shoulder and healing energy is flowing into it. Just ask."

So, I'm driving to physical therapy, chanting my mantra, visualizing white light up and down my right arm and shoulder. Jesus is in the passenger seat with his hand on my shoulder … and as the days passed, I am indeed feeling much, much better!

A couple of weeks before the scheduled surgery, the doc took more x-rays and told me that he didn't see a tear. No explanation given. The surgery was cancelled, and I was delighted. No problems since.

Wha' happened?

Was it the physical therapy? The mantra? White light? Positive thinking? Psychoendoneuroimmunology? Faith healing? Placebo effect? Jesus? None of the above? Some combination? Were the prayers answered? If so, which ones? A doctor attending one of my lectures offered this theory: the x-rays were probably mixed up or messed up and I actually had tendonitis.

I can't know for certain what catalyzed this outcome. What I *do* know was that I demonstrated a flexible belief system. I was willing to experiment with an open mind and positive attitude.

That's the factual data and the happy result. Draw your own conclusions.

BE INSPIRED—STAY INSPIRED!

When I think about *Man's Search For Meaning* by Viktor Frankl or *The Last Lecture* by Randy Pauch, or listen to recordings by The Beatles, Brian Wilson, Stevie Wonder ... when I see Shawn White snowboard ... when I think about my dad and mom's kindness or my wife's artistic ability—I'm INSPIRED!

- Inspired to believe that "I can do it also."

- Inspired to make my life just a little better than it is now.

- Inspired to refrain from complaining.

- Inspired to "do the right thing."

- Inspired to help others.

- Inspired to stop noshing on the "worry curry" and get on with it!

Extend the benefits that come from inspiration by remembering and reinforcing the inspiration-triggers.

Suggestion: Make a list.

I'M INSPIRED BY (people, books, music, etc.)

_____

_____

_____

_____

_____

Read and revise regularly (4-7 days a week)

Advanced version—

I'M INSPIRED BY _____
BECAUSE _____

I'M INSPIRED BY _____
BECAUSE _____

I'M INSPIRED BY _____
BECAUSE _____

I'M INSPIRED BY _____
BECAUSE _____

I'M INSPIRED BY _____
BECAUSE _____

I'M INSPIRED BY _____

BECAUSE _____

I'M INSPIRED BY _____

BECAUSE _____

SUGGESTION:

When you read a book, hear a lecture or watch a video that inspires you:

1. Write down the key points on a little card.

2. Look at the little card for a minute or two daily as you feel the feelings that energize you ... remember your goals ... vividly imagine the outcomes you desire most (and the steps necessary to achieve them), and enjoy!

3. Keep doing it. Create a collection of little cards.

4. Read those little cards every day. Pay close attention to what you're reading.

5. Daily. I mean it.

If this process, and similar techniques, seem a bit dorky to you, we'll just keep it between us. No one else has to know. It can be our secret.

But, will it work? Try it and see for yourself!

A SUPER-EASY WAY TO FOCUS ATTENTION—MAKE LISTS!

I love lists! They keep me on purpose, remind me of important things to do, and reinforce my motivations. Lists help me stay inspired, guide my actions and are certainly cost-effective. Lists are quintessential laborsaving devices! Lists get results!

You might have found it useful to keep a to-do list of errands you need to run, tasks you have to complete, and projects you need to work on. Generally, keeping a to-do list results in more accomplishments, and over time, a sense of which jobs are important to you ... and which aren't.

So the to-do list can provides some valuable feedback and increase self-awareness. For example, if I have something on my list from 1998, and I haven't checked if off yet ... is this a message for me? Is it possible that I just DON'T WANNA DO IT???? Or ... do I? What's going on here?

We often derive great pleasure and pride from the accomplishment of something on the list ... followed by the emotionally fulfilling cross-off and perhaps a high-five.

Tasks and accomplishments are just one area of life to manage.

What about emotions? Beliefs? Philosophies?

To better manage and create emotions, consider keeping a "to-feel" list. On that list, note the emotions you want to feel more of, such as: happy, secure, confident, and grateful. Maybe you want to feel calm, easy, successful, flexible, and smart. Make a list, review it daily, edit as necessary, and see what happens. By focusing attention on these things, you might make choices, and eventually develop habits of behavior and perception that support the emotional states you desire.

I also really like keeping a "to-remember" list. This one might have sayings, quotations, and even clichés that remind me to think, feel, and act in the ways I most desire to.

The to-remember list can help us ride the ups and downs of life with greater ease. Here are some examples:

TO REMEMBER

Change is part of life.

Appreciate the moment.

Notice the good things .

Each moment is a potential miracle .

Be kind.

Liberally and sincerely express gratitude and appreciation.

Make choices based on the outcomes I most desire.

Go with the flow.

Win some, lose some … still, if I'm breathing, I'm a winner!

"What, me worry?" (Alfred E. Newman)

This kind of simple daily reinforcement could catalyze miracles, help us reach our goals, improve relationships. It makes sense. Costs nothing. Doesn't take too much time. Nothing stopping you! So, do it, already. Put it on your list!

More Lists I Have Known and Loved

Lists draw my attention.

Tweak my selective perception.

Do you love synchronicities?

When you notice or participate in a good one, write it on a list.

You'll begin getting more of them, I reckon!

Do you have favorite quotations?

Make a Favorite Quotations List.

What do *you* think would happen if you made one—or more—of these lists, reviewed them weekly (at least), and revised as you see fit?

- Things That Make Me Happy

After asking an audience to write down "five things that make me happy," I asked them how it made them feel when they read their lists. Answers included:

> Happy (not a surprise)
>
> Joyous
>
> Excited

Peaceful

Calm

Grateful

Appreciative of the little things

Egotistical (*that* one made me think)

- Things I Do That Make Other People Happy
- Things I Definitely Want In My Life
- Things I Definitely Do NOT Want In My Life
- People I'm Grateful For
- Mistakes I'd Rather Not Repeat
- How I Want To Treat My (Family, Spouse, Customers, Coworkers)
- Food I Want To Avoid, Food I Want To Eat (two columns)
- Habits I Want To Make, Habits I Want To Break (also two columns)
- My Prime Directives

WHAT ABOUT DISAPPOINTMENT?

When we're learning a new skill—a new foreign language, playing a musical instrument, sports, positive thinking, gratitude-feeling, miracle-making or otherwise—there are bound to be mistakes, failures and disappointment. This is OK. We're not expected to be perfect—especially when we're at a beginning.

There is a learning curve. Be kind and patient with yourself.

"If you want a happy ending, that depends, of course, on where you stop your story."

Orson Welles

Realistic optimism, that's the ticket!

Does this sound familiar?

> You have unlimited potential.
>
> Imagine it ... and you can have it.
>
> You can have anything you want.
>
> You create your own reality.
>
> Allow the Universe to give you the abundance you deserve.

These might work better:

> You can increase the likelihood of success.

> You can imagine things, think things, and do things that are helpful.

> You can have a lot of what you want.

> You can make really good choices.

> You can notice and appreciate the abundance you already have.

Nonetheless, disappointment happens. Can disappointment be fuel for improvement? Maybe. Under certain circumstances. Perhaps. Could be.

When life gives you lemons, you could make lemonade (of course), then open an lemonade stand, franchise it, sell the business, take the proceeds and do what you really want to do with your life! Conversely, you could get some lemon juice in your eye, and cry, cry, and cry.

I'm disappointed because:

> I lost a job.

> I lost some money.

> I was lied to.

I trusted, now I'm humiliated.

I'm not where I think I could be.

I didn't get the love I deserved.

I was fooled.

I was rejected.

I was betrayed by a trusted friend.

My stocks crashed.

The restaurant got my order wrong.

It's raining.

My butt looks too big in these pants.

My children don't call me enough.

I don't like the way I look.

I have to pay more taxes then I thought.

The salesperson was rude to me.

The jerk in front of me has 14 items in
the 12-items-or-less line.

How Can I Feel?

Hurt.

Grateful for the blessings I have.

Uncomfortable.

Joyous that I remembered to keep a
rational perspective.

Depressed.

Weathered and beaten.

OK.

Motivated and inspired to move
forward.

Compassionate for others ... and myself.

Let the healing continue!

I can choose to forgive myself and the other. I
have options. I can seek a solution. I can take
the high road.

Or, I can pout like a child and feel kind of
crappy. I can get back into bed, pull the covers
over my head, cry over spilled milk, arrange a
pity-party, and eat way too much chocolate.
Actually, the chocolate doesn't sound all that
bad!

What can I learn about my risk tolerance?
About my choices? About myself?

DISAPPOINTMENT CAN BE A VALUED
AND RESPECTED TEACHER

"Do not lose your inner peace for anything
whatsoever, even if your whole world seems
upset."

Saint Francis de Sales

"A dead end street is a good place to turn around."

Naomi Judd

Are There Really Two Sides To Every Story?

I think there are more like "hundreds of sides" to every story.

Redundant Cliché Alert:

"What I see is determined by where I stand."

"Don't judge a book by its cover."

One of my favorite authors, the late Robert Anton Wilson, wrote about "reality tunnels"—that we see our own "reality" as if we were looking through a narrow tunnel—tunnel vision, as it is popularly called. He also used the abbreviation B.S. as in, "We all have our own B.S." Belief system, that is! Rest in peace, R.A.W. and thanks for writing so many thought-provoking, insightful books.

You may have seen or heard about a short film that shows two small teams of basketball players, one team wearing white shirts, the other wearing dark ones. The instructions are to watch the film and count how many passes of the basketballs the team wearing the white shirts makes. So we watch and count. What a majority of people DON'T see is the person in the full-body gorilla costume (a woman, I'm told), who walks into the frame, beats her chest, dances around a bit, and walks out.

Of course, not only are we focusing on the white-shirted players, and following the bouncing balls, we're tuning out the dark-shirted players, and the gorilla suit is also dark.

Inattentional blindness, as this phenomenon is often called.

What do we notice, what do we ignore?

What do we remember, what do we forget?

When I remind myself regularly of what I desire to notice, then I probably will see the gorilla.

Cliché alert:

"Never ascribe to malice that which is adequately explained by incompetence." (Attributed to Robert J. Hanlon, Robert A. Heinlein, Napoleon Bonaparte, probably others)

When I regularly put my attention on this saying, for example, I increase the probability of my remembering it ... and perhaps seeing things differently, interpreting events differently, and *feeling* differently when, instead of getting angry, I might demonstrate more compassion and patience.

Can I make my life better simply by looking at a little cliché every day? Seems to be the theme of *this* show!

How many motivational speakers does it take to change a light bulb? Just one, but the bulb has to really want to be inspired to create and allow the change.

BLIPS AND BITS

ALLOW

Allow yourself to honor the hero.

Allow yourself to avoid the bunko.

Allow yourself to forgive the bozo.

Allow yourself to release old cargo.

Allow yourself to perform with gusto.

Allow yourself to gather the info.

Allow yourself to enjoy the show.

Allow yourself to be in the know.

Allow yourself to become the maestro.

Great ideas keep coming.

Better write them down!

Take notes. Then ... read the notes.

Repeat.

So, you want to be enlightened?

"Strictly speaking there are no enlightened people, there is only enlightened activity."

Suzuki Roshi

"I enjoy feedback. Intelligence is function of feedback. The more feedback you get, the more intelligent you become. The less feedback you get, the stupider you become."

Robert Anton Wilson

Need a perspective shift?

"Just think how happy you would be if you lost everything you have right now, and then got it back again."

Attributed to Francis Rodman

"It's not what you look at that matters, it's what you see."

Henry David Thoreau

"Remember, today is the tomorrow you worried about yesterday."

Dale Carnegie

"I have the world's largest collection of seashells. I keep it on beaches all over the world."

Steven Wright

20 ALL-PURPOSE RESOLUTIONS

For New Year's and Otherwise

Pick your favorite reminders and review daily!

I WANT TO EVOLVE … AND SO I RESOLVE TO …

1. notice what's right in my world … and what needs fixing.

2. approach great ideas as tools, not just fine notions.

3. be here now. (Right place—right time—right mind)

4. observe my belief systems. Empowering or limiting?

5. make a list of what makes me happy. Read daily.

6. make a list of ways to make others happy. Read daily.

7. be flexible … but keep the backbone.

8. maximize kismet (make the most of chance opportunities).

9. ask myself "What really matters?" a few times daily.

10. think about people who inspire bravery and greatness.

11. awaken gratefully, hopefully, and delightedly.

12. exercise the skills of being helpful.

13. avoid grouchy posturing no matter what I'm thinking.

14. reverse direction before crossing the line.

15. remember: some miracles just take practice.

16. feel love and gratitude—express love and gratitude.

17. happily pay it forward.

18. treasure each moment, including this one.

19. use the word "impossible" with great caution.

20. make my choices based on the outcomes I most desire.

Gratitude and Mood Management Dept.

Be on the lookout for uplifting recordings that make you feel happy, inspire gratitude, stir positive emotions and put you in a good mood. Make your own list. Burn a CD. Create an iTunes playlist.

I call them "Grati-Tunes" (suggested by Sheila Elaine Brown. Thanks, Sheila!)

These are a few I've heard lately:

Thanks For The Memories—Bob Hope

Don't Worry, Be Happy—Bobby McFerrin

Thank You—Dido

Thank You—Led Zeppelin

What a Wonderful World—Louis Armstrong

'S Wonderful—George Gershwin (performed by many artists)

Thank You Girl—The Beatles

In My Life—The Beatles

Something—The Beatles

Here Comes the Sun—The Beatles

The End—The Beatles

Beautiful Boy—John Lennon

Maybe I'm Amazed—Paul McCartney

I Just Want to Celebrate—Rare Earth

Thank You (Falettinme Be Mice Elf Agin)—
Sly and the Family Stone

Be Thankful—Natalie Cole

I Thank You—Sam and Dave

Friends—The Beach Boys

How Sweet It Is—Marvin Gaye

To Sir With Love—Lulu

Pack Up Your Sorrows—Mimi and Richard
Fariña

Thanks to XM/Sirius Satellite Radio and
Pandora Internet Radio—two true miracles!

Jot down a few of your own favorites …

_____

_____

_____

_____

_____

DOES LOVE TRUMP EVERYTHING?

_____ YES

_____ NO

_____ SOMETIMES

_____ MAYBE

_____ DEPENDS

_____ AS MUCH AS POSSIBLE

_____ HELL, YEAH!

_____ AS LONG AS LOVE IS FAIR

_____ MAKES SENSE

_____ I TRIED LOVE ONCE, GOT BURNED, DECIDED NEVER AGAIN

_____ WHAT, EXACTLY DO YOU MEAN BY "LOVE"

_____ NOT SURE

The results of expanded love-awareness and expression, can be:

> Healing
>
> Life-changing
>
> Nurturing
>
> Educational
>
> Miracle-provoking

Fun

Hep, hip, cool, and groovy

Not all that difficult

Did I mention life-changing?

Love is a noun and love is a verb.

1. Recognizing Love (as a noun), and
2. Demonstrating Love, (as a verb).

Love comes in many flavors, textures, and shapes!

Sincerely and liberally express it.

Don't wait … do it today.

Over time, I have strongly suspected that love trumps

money … "stuff" … pettiness … malarkey … bullshit … complaining … worry … arguing and fighting … self-pity … mishegas … insecurities …. the small, sometimes annoying, bumps in the road.

SO … perhaps we DO want to CHOOSE MORE LOVE!

IT'S POSSIBLE.

WHAT FORMS OF LOVE DO YOU WANT?

Security? Partnership? Affection? Abundance?

Caring? Nurturing? Comfort? Happiness?

WHAT FORMS OF LOVE DO YOU WANT TO GIVE MORE OF?

Clear communications? Sharing? Affection? Service with a smile?

Caring? Nurturing actions? Comfort? Compassion? Good moods? Cookies?

Try these reminders on for size. Put a ✓ next to the one or ones that you agree with:

_____ I can allow more and more love into my life.

_____ Love often dissolves insecurity.

_____ Love trumps everything.

_____ I can express love sincerely, liberally, and appropriately.

_____ I honor my own process of becoming more loving!

_____ I can end my own "anti-love" habits and patterns.

_____ I can put love into my work.

_____ I can recognize that people do love me.

_____ I can feel the love.

_____ I deserve love and so do others.

_____ I can become more loving in my relationships.

_____ I love stuff like this!

Love is the glue for me and you.

Love is the light that dissolves the fright.

Why not appreciate the love, bask in the love, take showers in the love, do the polka in the love, play dominos in the love, and _be_ the love? Yes! Be the love you want to see!

Stop the blaming! Consign blame to the maybe state. Sometimes we find out that we've incorrectly placed the blame. Then what? An emotional mess to clean up! Try kindness and compassion instead (for others _and yourself_).

Every thought matters. You are the creator in your own unique universe, and your THOUGHTS are the triggers for enlightened behavior and actions … or the opposite. So … remember to think delightful thoughts of love! Regularly. Over and out!

How do I love thee?

How do I love thee?
Let me count the ways.

Elizabeth Barrett Browning

Here are 20 of them:

1. By being kind to you.

2. By understanding you.

3. By having fun with you.

4. By being myself with you.

5. By not martyring myself.

6. By managing my moods before they manage our relationship.

7. With gratitude and forgiveness.

8. By making my choices based on the outcomes we desire most.

9. By honoring our tremendous good fortune, daily.

10. With honesty.

11. Presents in the present.

12. Demonstrations of affection and appreciation.

13. Solid commitment.

14. Consideration of your feelings.

15. Respectfully.

16. With a sense of humor.

17. Patience.

18. Great meals.

19. Flexibility.

20. With pleasure.

LOVE IS GOOD TEAMWORK IN ACTION.

Adaptive, responsive and empathic.

Advocating fairness, honesty, unity, and loyalty.

Responsive, not reactive!

The Emotional Affectionate Miracle

Do you want to align your intentions with:

The TEAM or the Petty Annoyance Alliance?

The TEAM or the I'll Never Get What I Want Club?

The TEAM or MartyrCorp?

So, if love is so great, how do I get more of it?

1. Give more of it.

2. Write a daily Love Journal—by listing five:

   - loving thoughts

   - people who have ever shown me love or demonstrated love

   - examples of love in my life

- things I love, etc.

3. Say "I love you" with feeling.

4. Communicate kindly: verbally and nonverbally.

5. Visualize (mentally rehearse) yourself experiencing the love you desire.

6. Visualize yourself solving conflicts, not avoiding them.

7. Remember that love is a noun *and* a verb.

8. Create it, generate it, project it, live in it.

9. Expect it. Allow it. Choose it.

"And the day came when the risk it took to remain tight inside the bud was more painful than the risk it took to blossom."

Anaïs Nin

Old Dogs Can Learn New Tricks

Today, I washed the breakfast dishes, cleaned the coffeemaker and straightened up the kitchen automatically, absent-mindedly, and I'm happy to report, efficiently. As I observed myself finishing up, I had to laugh.

As a long-time bachelor, I NEVER did any kitchen chores, much less cooked for myself. It was either eat-out or take-out, all the time. My apartment kitchen was primarily used for storage. I didn't have any use for the stove, so I had the gas disconnected back in '93. The oven was home to small musical instruments.

When I married Lynne in 2007, and began to experience daily life with an active, working kitchen, I was, to say the least, clueless—unconsciously incompetent. I didn't even know how to properly slice an apple (she still likes to tell that story—my results were quite creative). I had no idea where anything was kept, nor the ability to identify the difference between *saucepan* and *cakepan*. Frankly, this bugged me. It was frustrating, like the first day on a new job with no training.

I needed to learn, and I did. Little by little, I began to "get it."

I was becoming proud of my newly acquired abilities to know which bowl was which, and how to prepare string beans for steaming. But four years later, I do what needs to be done, without instruction or being asked to, inhabiting the wonderful state of unconscious competence—i.e., habit.

The path of mastery seems like a common-sense process to me. Practice. Attention. Patience. Trial and error. Feedback. Good coaching and mentoring. Compassion for the student and the teacher. All fueled by the desire to master the tasks. I'm still not a perfect kitchen worker, but I *am* averaging a B+ in "Practical Home Ec 101."

Doesn't it feel great when you've been diligently practicing—skills, behaviors, cooking, dishwashing—and you realize that you're doing it flawlessly … and automatically? I love that!

"Never, never, never give up."

Winston Churchill

"We learn by practice. Whether it means to learn to dance by practicing dancing or to learn to live by practicing living, the principles are the same."

Martha Graham

"It's kind of fun to do the impossible."

Walt Disney

Let Bygones Be Bygones

A few words about unwanted grudges …

Let them go.

Life is short.

Anger is worse for the grudger than for the grudgee.

Perhaps "forgive and forget" is a little extreme? OK.

I'm sticking with "let it go."

Lose the grudge.

And … let the healing begin!

Use The All-Purpose FORGIVENESS TOOL

Forgiveness for my own worst mistakes,

forgiveness to the neighbor who forgets to return my rake.

Forgiveness for dads, moms, sisters, brothers,

forgiveness for bad bosses and stock market losses.

Forgiveness for my own human imperfections,

forgiveness for abandonments and rejections.

Who gets FORGIVEN?

Mama and Daddy-O,

Moi,

Friends,

Some enemies, too,

Loved ones who died,

The good people I've rejected,

The good people who've rejected me.

Knuckleheads and goofballs,

Insecure shrinking violets and insecure control
freaks,

People who fooled me,

Offspring, siblings, queens, and kings,

Drama geeks, uncomfortable bedsprings,

Lousy bosses, double crosses (very
challenging),

The wayward humiliator,

The prideful vindicator,

The uncaring service provider,

The woman in ghastly attire.

Everyone else, if I want.

That just about covers it.

Why FORGIVE?

It transforms *every* relationship! That's right! Just *one* act of forgiveness sets the famed butterfly effect into motion, and *all* relationships are given a positive boost.

It makes you feel really great!

It is excellent karma.

It changes mental focus, putting things into a more workable perspective, sometimes triggering fits of cosmic enlightenment along with uninhibited happy-dancing!

Just goes to show you just how much transformational power you really do have!

FORGIVENESS PROMOTES LOVE

WAYS TO PARTICIPATE IN THE GREAT FORGIVENESS:

1. Get a little card and write, "I love and forgive _____.

Fill in the blank with the name of the person you'd most like to forgive and love. Read the card three times daily. FEEL the forgiveness as you read it. You can certainly omit the word "love" if you'd like. But love is a pretty good feeling to practice, so you might as well just leave it in.

2. Think: FIX, NOT FAULT.

3. Go easy on the drama.

4. Repeat this Stuart-Smalley-sounding mantra for two or three minutes, two or three times daily: *I forgive myself. My self forgives me. Others forgive me and I accept it.* Another one: *I am an electrode of love and forgiveness.*

5. Remember that I sometimes project my own nonsense on the "movie screens" of others and that it just might be a good idea to stop it.

6. Pretend that you are truly and finally forgiven for all your blunders, and that your job on Earth is to forgive everyone else for theirs. This is just a pretend exercise; please don't debate me on this one. Thank you!

Can Your Brain Use A Software Upgrade?

Know what you want,

work for what you want,

ask for help with what you want,

and you just might get it!

If you'd like to tweak, modify, install, or delete a few habitual thought patterns, then the following exercise will probably help. Takes five or six minutes a day. Easy!

Try it daily for 30 days.

THE DAILY AWARENESS
EXERCISE—IN TWO STEPS

STEP ONE: Read and ponder the following six phrases:

1. There are ways that I can remember and practice points of view, behaviors, beliefs, and actions that give optimal results, especially when I know what results I'm seeking.

2. I can evaluate my own beliefs and habits with compassion and a cool head.

3. I can make changes as necessary, especially when my desire is clear and strong.

4. I see the wisdom in liberally expressing gratitude and appreciation.

5. It is possible for me to evaluate feedback without becoming defensive.

6. I can have some fun every day; it will probably make me less annoying.

STEP TWO: Write for three or four minutes.

Any ideas and feelings that come to you as a result of considering the phrases in Step One … write or type them. Keep a running journal. At least three full minutes of writing— uncensored.

Am I seeing the gorilla now? Noticing the elephant in the room?

More Posi-Blips

Digging into the archives … (from Jerry's 1993 journal at age 40)

Life is an all-you-can-eat buffet.

Choose wisely.

Learn to recreate yourself … for fun … and profit!

We have our internal radio stations—sometimes there's heavy interference.

Who (or what) is broadcasting on your own internal mind channels?

Get your own Inner Emotional Team in line, so you're not battling yourself.

Self-pity? Perfectionism? Inappropriate anger? Feelings of overwhelm? Feel 'em … and *heal* 'em!

I am in the prison of my own creation and I have the key in my pocket.

Billboards behind my head—proclaiming my feelings to the world!

Life is a multitrack tape and we're doing the mixing.

Do your thoughts do one thing while your feelings do another?

Resist the gravity of the irrelevant stuff.

Let the love in. Now.

STILL MORE LOVE STUFF

"If your head tells you one thing and your heart tells you another, before you do anything, you should first decide whether you have a better head or a better heart."

Marilyn Vos Savant

"The meeting of two personalities is like the contact of two chemical substances: if there is any reaction, both are transformed."

Carl Jung

"Love is everything it's cracked up to be...It really is worth fighting for, being brave for, risking everything for."

Erica Jong

Loving someone is an excellent reason to communicate clearly. Precisely.

Say what you mean, mean what you say, and don't say it mean!

The loved one (and everyone else for that matter) reads the nuances of communication:

> choice of words,
>
> body language,

and especially ... TONE!

That data is then:

   interpreted,

   processed,

   and responded / reacted to.

Communications style, skill, and awareness affects:

   the relationship,

   your endocrine system, the endocrine
      systems of others

   and, of course, the Universe.

Poor communications often cause unnecessary pain!

Clear, accurate, kind communications are:

   smart,

   cost- and time-effective,

   and evolutionary!

MAGICAL LOVE SCRIPTS

Try these on your loved ones!

I love you very much.

I miss you when we're apart.

I understand you.

Our love makes me happy.

I love you, you're the best! Thank you for EVERYTHING!!!

My heart, soul & spirit ... they are all yours.

Great idea! Glad you mentioned it! Thanks for the excellent advice!

My love for you is greater than ever.

DEFENSIVE? ME? Yeah, I guess I was being a little defensive.

Your patience makes all the difference in the world.

You talk, I'll listen.

Your love for me is my rock, strength ... and my joy!

You were right. I'm sorry. I apologize.

LEARNING THE CODES

We come to every relationship with our individual communication codes and styles already in place. It's a miracle that we can understand each other at all!

Since the communications are coded, we might sometimes APPEAR TO THE LISTENER to be sending conflicting, confusing, or vague messages. I've heard it said that, "all communications are a gamble."

Learn the code-keys to unlock the context, intent, and mood of the speaker.

To ascertain the code-keys, consider:

> Listening (tone, speed, pitch, timbre)
>
> Watching (body language, non-verbal)
>
> Paying attention (content, context)
>
> Asking questions in a genuine and calm tone of voice
>
> Remembering what you learned last time!

LEARNING THE CODES IS AN ACT OF LOVE!

"The times I decide to see everyone as a teacher, I sure do learn a lot!"

> *JDP*

"I don't know what anything 'is' ... I only know how it seems to me at this moment."

> *Robert Anton Wilson*

"Reality is nothing but a collective hunch."

> *Lily Tomlin*

CREATE NEW CODES.

Invent a secret handshake.

Make up words, agree on the meanings.

Create guidelines, write down some rules.

THE LOVE THAT TRUMPS EVERYTHING *AWARENESS MAGIC*

"Perhaps the feelings that we experience when we are in love represent a normal state. Being in love shows a person who he should be."

Anton Chekhov

"There is no remedy for love but to love more."

Henry David Thoreau

"Love is an exploding cigar we willingly smoke."

Lynda Barry

At various times and stages of life, (and with continually shifting emphasis) we experience different varieties of love:

- The love of parents, relatives, extended family, community

- The love of being fed, nurtured, cared for, accepted

- The love of independence and freedom

- The love of friends, partners, pets, plants

- Philosophy, ideas, literature

- Stuff, things, financial security

- Sexual love, emotional intimacy, romance

- Recognition, accomplishment, success, winning

- Music, art, creative expression, job, work, career

- Spiritual love, humanitarian love, selfless love, love of service

- Love of personal growth, education, positive transformation

- Love of spouse, significant other, girlfriend / boyfriend

When we experience love / recognize love / accept love / create love:

- we're happy

- we're peaceful (or excited, or both at the same time!)

- we're grateful

- we feel connected

- congratulations are in order!

- our immune systems probably work more efficiently

- we glow

- we treat people with more kindness, compassion, and patience.

- we're satisfied

What forms of love are most important in your life right now? Get a small card (file card or business card) and jot down the first three that come to mind. In other words, what kinds of love do you want?

1.

_____

2.

_____

3.

_____

- Then, read the card three times daily and think about it.

- Write a new card every week (even if your list is the same).

- Do something about it.

- Repeat.

HANDY ACRONYMS

L. A. F. F.

Love. Action. Fairness. Forgiveness.

Listen. Apologize. Fix it. Follow Up.

T. A. C .O.

Thoughts. Attitudes. Communications. Observations.

A. I. M.

Attitude. Impact. Motivation.

S. N. I. P.

Stop Negativity I Perceive.

Skip Nonsense, Ignite Potential.

K.I.S.S.

Keep It Simple, Sweetheart!

21 MORE ALL-PURPOSE HELPFUL REMINDERS

1. Anticipate life's tests and the best ways to pass them.

2. Compassion is always an option.

3. Confidence just might stack the odds in my favor.

4. Express curiosity instead of becoming defensive.

5. Return all phone calls. Yes, all of them.

6. Make my mom proud.

7. Say "you're welcome" instead of "no problem."

8. Am I worrying for nothing … again?

9. Moment-to-moment appreciation and gratitude.

10. A great answer: "I don't know, but I will find out."

11. Two more great ones: "It depends." "You never know."

12. Think twice before broadcasting sarcasm.

13. Every eye-roll and frown sends a message.

14. Every smile sends a message, too.

15. Look for the miracles in everyday life.

16. Avoid superstitions … unless they work, of course!

17. Synchronize communication codes.

18. Ask myself, "What do I keep, what do I throw away?"

19. Notice and thank the angels amongst us.

20. Know what I want most and act accordingly.

21. Wisdom works better when applied daily.

Universal Love

Universal Love trumps the lack of it.

I've always wanted to get the knack of it!

Universal Love includes everyone ...is lots of fun ... gets the job done!

"Love all, trust a few. Do wrong to none."

William Shakespeare, "All's Well That Ends Well", Act 1 Scene 1

Universal Love is always here:

- to experience

- to broadcast

- to bask in

- to share

- to enjoy

Universal Love can trigger peace, harmony, good decisions, magical outcomes.

Fortunately, Love-awareness can be accessed at any time.

The "resonance" or "vibrations" or "feelings" of Love often promote:

- smart decision-making
- devotion to higher principles and ethics
- a sense of emotional security
- enhanced spirituality
- that "tingly" sensation
- maturity, growth, improvement "across the board"!
- definitely more fun.

Personal Love wants the best ... makes people feel blest ... passes the tests.

Spiritual Love makes good karma ... promotes the dharma ... is a phenom'na!

Philosophical Love is wide and deep ... not too bad before you drift off to sleep.

Love of Music takes us places ... sonic embraces, trebles, and basses.

Universal Love contains it all ... an emotional and psychospiritual windfall!

"He who is in love is wise and is becoming wiser, sees newly every time he looks at the object beloved, drawing from it with his eyes and his mind those virtues which it possesses."

Ralph Waldo Emerson

"Before I met my husband, I'd never fallen in love, though I'd stepped in it a few times."

Rita Rudner

"Can absence make the heart grow fonder? I say, 'Why wait?'"

JDP

YO, LOVERAP

Say it "Love Rap" or "Lover App"

Application that is, 'cause practicality is my biz!

Or the appetizer that makes us wiser!

Here's a map to unwrap the flap and cut through the crap.

It's not too late to elate the irate primates!

Bumps in the road

are part of the course.

some relationships are strengthened ...

some, headed for divorce!

Does my love trump the bump

or does the bump trump?

That is the question.

What's my intention?

Love takes a chance ...

Love takes a stance

to advance the romance —

and enhance the circumstance.

How much is luck and how much skill?
It's an ample gamble to install the love thrill!
Our union is no illusion or delusion ...
the inclusion feels like nuclear fusion!

Let the future be better than your past.
Focus on the outcomes that you want to last.
Potentials are vast.
Real love is unsurpassed!
(I've become a steadfast enthusiast!)

Wisdom in a Word

And our audience said …

Gratitude.

Empathize.

Compassion.

Share.

Nurture.

Think.

Appreciate.

Love.

Exhale.

Humility.

Smile.

Selfless.

Reflect.

Humor.

Breathe.

Silence.

Relax.

Be.

"To play it safe is not to play."

Robert Altman

"I am always doing things I can't do; that's how I get to do them."

Pablo Picasso

"Address your audience, not yourself."

Good Advice

Today, Positive Reality Theatre would like to present

a short musical, entitled:

What's In YOUR Reality?

Please turn off all cell phones and pagers before the show begins.

Thank you, and ... enjoy the show!

The curtain rises. One by one, the players walk to center stage, pause, bow, and take their places.

Entire Cast:

We play the part!

Positive realities a la carte!

The Old Professor With A Twinkle In His Eye:

What images and scenes do YOU reinforce

in your own, private 'reality theaters'?

Hmmmmmmm?

Altos & Sopranos:

What would that look like to you?

Does it make you happy, or make you blue?

Does it make my life a prison ...

or a magic land of love?

Why can't I make decisions,

that fit my ambitions like a glove?

Basses, Baritones & Tenors:

You can.

You can.

You caaaaaaaaaaaaannnnnnnnnnnnnn.

Sally Von Becker:

Does it make my life blissful ...

on a boring sort of day?

Steve Von Becker:

Honey, with your love in my life,

every day is a holiday!

Sally Von Becker:

Awwwwww, Chuck ... I mean, Steve!

Haha ha. Just kidding! You mean the world to me.

Altos & Sopranos:

Awwwwww!

Adorable!

Cute!

We like it!

Al Foonman (spoken):

So a miracle transpired, I fell in love.

A love so right that I couldn't deny it!

Altos & Sopranos:

He couldn't deny it!

Oh yeah!

Al Foonman (spoken):

My bachelor days were mostly happy.

Or so I thought.

But now. But now! BUT NOW!!!!!!

Wowie zowie!

Talk about positive realities!

This one trumps everything!

Everyone:

Love (la la la la la)

trumps (ooh ooh ooh ooh)

everything … everything … everything … boop-boop-a-doop … yeah!

CURTAIN

Announcer

Thanks for coming! We certainly hope you had a good time! Don't forget to tip your server and drive safely! Adios!

Practicing the Practical Power of Gratitude

"Gratitude unlocks the fullness of life. It turns what we have into enough, and more."
Melody Beattie

"I would maintain that thanks are the highest form of thought; and that gratitude is happiness doubled by wonder."

G.K. Chesterton

"He is a wise man who does not grieve for the things which he has not, but rejoices for those which he has."

Epictetus

More and more, I'm reading academic research and scientific studies linking happiness to gratitude. This is pretty much a no-brainer: the more gratitude and thankfulness I feel, the happier I become. The more appreciation I express to others, the more happiness I spread. I don't think we need too much research here—seems like obvious common sense to me.

But common sense without practice isn't very practical … or powerful!

Practicing strongly suggests doing something—not just once or twice, but repeatedly. Eventually making skills or habits—habits of behavior, habits of thinking, habits of feeling, interpretation, perception, etc.

You've heard the cliché "practice makes perfect." Well, practice doesn't make perfect ... practice makes habits! Repeatedly practice something the "wrong" way, and you get very good at doing something wrong! For example, you might know some folks who are absolute masters of negative thinking ... self-pity ... self-sabotage ...

So, with regard to gratitude, what to practice?

1. FEELING GRATEFUL for the good things, the love, the laughs, the lessons, the people, the opportunities, the help, the stuff, the miracles, the food, the music, the technology, etc.

2. EXPRESSING GRATITUDE for the good things, the love, the laughs, the lessons, the people, the opportunities, the help, the stuff, the miracles, the food, the music, the technology, etc.

How do you FEEL when you feel grateful?

Happy? Peaceful? Blessed? Centered? Generous? Secure? Calm? Connected?

Good?

Thinking and expressing thankful thoughts, and amplifying feelings of gratitude, can reduce stress ... improve relationships ... and minimize pettiness! Beginning a dinner or business meeting by going around the table and having everyone mention something they're grateful for or happy about, can have significant positive impact.

You can't lose with gratitude!

Sincerely thank your customers, coworkers, friends, and family. Thank your vendors, suppliers, supporters, and fans! Be generous with your gratitude. Do it today. Do it all year round!

Write yourself some gratitude-oriented focus phrases (reminders) on cards and sticky-notes, and put them where you'll see them every day. We NEED reminders! We're human. We forget! We get distracted!

For example:

I CHOOSE TO EXPRESS GRATITUDE SINCERELY, GENEROUSLY AND LIBERALLY.

I EASILY AND REGULARLY GIVE THANKS.

I FEEL GRATEFUL FOR ALL OF MY GIFTS AND BLESSINGS.

EXPRESSING GRATITUDE MAKES ME FEEL GOOD—SO I DO IT!

Here's a fun and potentially enlightening "grati-tool"—make a list of 10 people who have helped you get to where you are right now—10 people you're grateful for. Ten people who helped you succeed, taught you important lessons, loved you.

1.

2.

3.

4.

5.

6.

7.

8.

9.

10.

We might be reminded of that thoughtful childhood neighbor who baked the best cookies, or a high school guidance counselor whose caring changed the course of our life. When we remember how kind and generous people have been in our lives, we might be inspired to pass it on, or "pay it forward." We might even reclaim some memories of our personal history that we'd forgotten. And ... it just might make us feel happier! Revisit your list from time to time (weekly, perhaps), and keep adding to it.

So, thank the people! Show some appreciation for them. Send thank-you notes. Tell the people you love that you love them. Don't wait until it's too late. Maybe you can bake some cookies for someone!

Another way to practice the practical power of gratitude is a one-minute stress-buster—THE GRATITUDE BREAK. First, select something specific about your life that you are truly, deeply thankful for (person, condition, or thing). Something or someone that you feel genuinely happy about. Then ... close your eyes (not while you're driving, please) and spend just one minute thinking about, and vividly imagining (if you can), that person, condition, or thing. FEEL the gratitude and happiness as you visualize!

Try a gratitude break once a day, and see what happens! Twice a day would be an interesting experiment.

A favorite "grati-tool" is THE GRATITUDE JOURNAL (a.k.a. "Five Good Things"). Here's what to do: every day (that would be DAILY), write down or type five things you are grateful for. They can be deep ... shallow ... serious ... funny ... spiritual ... material. Just list five things you're grateful for on paper or computer. Not in your head. Write them down.

1.

2.

3.

4.

5.

My friend David Starfield, who's had excellent results with this practice, suggests, "It's okay to repeat things, just be sincere." Good guideline. Specific is better than general ... but general is better than nothing!

Your mileage may vary! People who write a daily gratitude journal often report improved relationships, less stress, more patience, better decision-making, feeling more secure … and a greater sense of well being.

During challenging times, regular focus on gratitude can restore much needed balance. Not to deny that there might be adversity or challenges, but to remember that there are always wonderful things, too.

Practice the practical power of gratitude, and make every day a day of thanks-giving.

So many benefits … so small a cost!

To Assume Means ... Well, You Know!

"Don't worry, it will come back."

My dad's take on the financial crisis of 2008

Comedian and banjo player Steve Martin used to do a routine where he gets angrier and angrier because "someone stole my fifty dollars." He says that he knows his money was stolen because he always kept it in THIS pocket ... not the other pocket, which is where he embarrassingly discovers his money, of course.

All that anger for nothing!

So, why assume the worst? Why borrow anger, frustration, and pain from a potential future, one where they might not even exist?

Why make assumptions without sufficient information? Imaginary crisis and presumed wrongdoings result in very real feelings, which can further result in no good for anyone.

"Never attribute to malice that which is adequately explained by stupidity."

Hanlon's Razor, attributed to Robert J. Hanlon

For more years than I'd like to admit, my mood tracked with the ups and downs of the Dow Jones Industrial Average. But when I look back, the eternal cosmic wisdom of "win some, lose some" surely applied. I didn't really need all that emotional drama, and it took some focused awareness and discipline to break that habit of worry for nothing.

How about the student who agonizes, panics, and acts out the "woe is me, I'm going to fail" soliloquy before every exam, and gets an A anyway?

To break this unwanted habit, I regularly asked myself: "Have I been here before, and what happened?" The answers were: "yes, most every day" and "actually, nothing too bad ever happened."

This worked for me, and might work for you as well.

If we must make assumptions, why not positive, constructive ones?

By the way … in my stock portfolio? I always came out ahead anyway.

"Time goes by so fast, people go in and out of your life. You must never miss the opportunity to tell these people how much they mean to you."

From the last episode of "Cheers"

"It's always worthwhile to make others aware of their worth."

Malcolm Forbes

The Jerry Posner Radio Show—

Missing You When You're Not Here

MUSIC: "Jetsons Intro"—fades under …

JERRY: OK … As we were discussing before the break … I never looked forward to saying good-bye. Really didn't like good-byes! (sung) Never can say goodbye … never can say goodbye … la la la doo doo doo dooo! Haha ha ha! Anyway … I've come to understand that missing a loved one can be quite appropriate, and not necessarily a bad thing. How about you? How does your brain process it? Thoughts on the missing circuit? Yeah, the missing circuit. Let's discuss. We have Pookie from Minneapolis on the line. Pookie, how are you doing?

POOKIE: Good, thanks. You?

JERRY: If I were any better, I'd be twins. So, what's on your mind?

POOKIE: Is it a MISSING circuit or a missing CIRCUIT?

JERRY: It can be both. It can be that the circuit isn't activated (missing) .... and/or ... it can refer specifically to the circuit dedicated to processing "emotional energy associated with feelings of absence or lack."

POOKIE: Hmmmmmm. Thanks ... I guess.

JERRY: My pleasure! Next we have Bob from Thousand Oaks, California. Hi, Bob, and welcome.

BOB: Hi. So ... I had issues. ISSUES! I'm a busy guy, so my attention was on my work. But maybe I was kinda like a narcissist. And things ... situations ... always change anyway, right? Why get your knickers in a twist over that? Things change, we adapt, we get it and we get over it, you know what I mean?

JERRY: Yeah?

BOB: We're all human, right? Hi, mom!

JERRY: Thanks, Bob, and keep up the great work! Lynne is on the phone from Amsterdam. Hi, honey!

LYNNE: Hi, sweetheart! I miss you!

JERRY: I miss you, too! You'll never guess what today's show is about!

LYNNE: Let me guess. Might it be the usual emotional hoopla?

JERRY: Yep! What advice do you have for the ladies when their husbands or boyfriends are away ... on a business trips or something like that?

LYNNE: First, speak to him on the phone twice a day. Make the call pleasant ... not a gripe session or pity-party. Email every morning, first thing. A 'good morning, darling' message. Express your love, freely and honestly. Write things like: I love you passionately, ecstatically, permanently, and completely! And video chat on the iPad2 or Skype, fabulous!

JERRY: Oh, yeah! Excellent! And no snap judgments, based on phone or email. It is too easy for noise to interfere with the signal that you intend to send, causing the "misunderstanding response" and the anger, hurt, and annoyance that could go with it! And guys ... keep it sweet and affectionate. The tone of voice is VERY important—often the deal-maker OR the deal-breaker!

LYNNE: You're right about the tone! Gotta go now. I'll call you tomorrow! Love you!

JERRY: Love YOU!

FOCUS-PHRASES TO CONNECT WITH THOSE WE MISS

Love: the steadfast commitment to your well-being.

You are always here, in my heart and in my mind.

I am grateful for our relationship.

My life is better because of you.

I feel the connection with you, beyond time and space.

By missing you, my love deepens and becomes more evident.

Take Your Own Best Advice

I once attended a roundtable meeting for speakers and trainers at a local community college. One discussion topic was: What do you do when the unexpected happens? For example, what if your handouts, which were shipped ahead of time, didn't arrive. What if the audience size is thrice what you expected?

I offered the group some common sense cliché-like standards:

"Do the best you can, and don't worry about it."

"Improvise."

"Keep cool and flexible."

That evening, I arrived for a speaking gig to find that that the lock on my briefcase was jammed. So I didn't have access to the handouts and props that were integral to my lecture.

Ironic.

Instead of panic, which at the time would have been standard operating procedure, I decided that I would do the best I could, improvise and keep cool and flexible.

The presentation was one of my all-time best.

So, when you face a problem situation, ask yourself, "what advice would I give to someone else in this predicament?"

Then, take your own advice. If it works, write it down and perhaps someday, publish it in a book.

"Advice is what we ask for when we already know the answer but wish we didn't."

Erica Jong

"Whatever advice you give, be brief."

Horace

"In three words I can sum up everything I've learned about life: it goes on."

Robert Frost

BY THE WAY ...

"Be kind whenever possible. It is always possible."

Dalai Lama

"I may not have gone where I intended to go, but I think I have ended up where I needed to be."

Douglas Adams

"There are two ways to spread happiness; either be the light who shines it or be the mirror who reflects it."

Edith Wharton

"Despise not small things, either for evil or good, for a look may work thy ruin, or a word create thy wealth. A spark is a little thing, yet it may kindle the world.

Martin Farquhar Tupper

"Life is what we make it. Always has been, always will be."

Grandma Moses

"It's so simple to be wise. Just think of something stupid to say and then don't say it."

Sam Levenson

And a few more of those wise old sayings:

Every picture tells a story.

Two wrongs don't make a right.

Necessity is the mother of invention.

Garbage in … garbage out. (GIGO)

Better safe than sorry.

It takes two to tango.

Look before you leap.

One good turn deserves another.

You can't please everyone.

Yesterday is history. Tomorrow is a mystery. Today is a gift; that's why they call it the present.

Thank You!

Well dear reader, we made it to the end! I hope you had a good time and got some useful ideas. Jot down the ones you REALLY want to remember, on little cards perhaps, and read 'em daily!

I could go on and on, especially about gratitude, but that will probably be a focus of the next book.

Until then …

Remember, practice doesn't make perfect. Practice makes habits. So, be aware of what you're practicing!

Write your gratitude journal.

Express unconditional kindness.

Compassion is always an option.

Everything affects everything.

Love trumps everything.

Reinforce the positive sayings of your choice.

Be a conscious wisdom collector. After all, everyone needs a hobby!

Collect great ideas, inspiring quotations, food for thought.

A nice, inexpensive hobby!

Evolution can be fun!

Sincere best wishes,

Jerry

When the cellist Pablo Casals was in his early 90s, he was asked by a student, "Master, why do you continue to practice?" Casals replied, "Because I am making progress."

ABOUT THE AUTHOR

Jerry Posner is an engaging speaker, writer, "motivational entertainer," and ukulele player. After a near-death experience in 1976, he set upon a lifelong quest to learn and practice ways to become a more positive, growth-oriented, productive and, well, happier person. He takes a practical, open-minded, and fun approach to self-improvement and self-mastery, sharing his stories and research with diverse (and appreciative) audiences.

After working in radio (including program director of an all-comedy station near Los Angeles in the 80s), he and his partners published the *Positive Times Journal* in the 90s. Jerry was the commercial voice of the "Great Russian Nutcracker" ballet company for many years, and still voices and produces the occasional radio commercial.

He's been a popular guest lecturer at Canyon Ranch in Lenox, MA since 1993, presenting programs such as "Ways To Create Miracles In Your Life," "Practicing the Practical Power of Gratitude," and "Ways To Make 'The Butterfly Effect' Work For You."

Jerry has presented workshops and seminars for a wide variety of clients, including: GE Plastics, Berkshire Life Insurance, Diversified Agency Services at Omnicom Group,

Distinctive Hospitality Group, Smith Barney, Merrill Lynch, Brunswick Corp., Aubuchon Hardware, Crowne Plaza Hotels, Tio Juan's Margaritas Restaurants (NH, ME, CT, MA, NJ), National Endowment for the Arts, Federal Deposit Insurance Corporation (Boston and NYC), Berkshire Bank, and AppleMetro, Inc.

Jerry is the author of *Attention Late Bloomers: You're Right On Time!*

Raised in Northern New Jersey, he attended Emerson College in Boston, graduating magna cum laude with a degree in mass communications. He lives in Massachusetts, with his wife Lynne, Max the Labrador, and Ruby the Vizsla.

For more about Jerry, and booking information, please visit www.jerryposner.com

His blog: http://jerryposner.wordpress.com/

His LinkedIn page: http://www.linkedin.com/in/jerryposner

If you'd like, "friend" him on Facebook, and you'll observe "Grati-Tuesdays" together!

14131576R00075

Made in the USA
Charleston, SC
22 August 2012